All About Dinosaurs

Brachiosaurus

Daniel Nunn

Heinemann
LIBRARY
Chicago, Illinois

© 2015 Heinemann Library
an imprint of Capstone Global Library, LLC
Chicago, Illinois

To contact Capstone Global Library, please
call 800-747-4992, or visit our web site
www.capstonepub.com

Edited by Daniel Nunn and James Benefield
Designed by Tim Bond
Picture research by Tracy Cummins
Production by Helen McCreath
Originated by Capstone Global Library Ltd
Printed in the United States of America in
North Mankato, MN. 112014 008608RP

Library of Congress Cataloging-in-Publication Data
Nunn, Daniel, author.
  Brachiosaurus / Daniel Nunn.
    pages cm.—(All about dinosaurs)
  Summary: "This book takes a very simple look at the
Brachiosaurus dinosaur, examining what it looked
like, what it ate, how it behaved, and its special skills
and features such as its very long neck. The book also
discusses how we know about Brachiosaurus today,
showing where fossils are found and how scientists put
them together."—Provided by publisher.
  Includes bibliographical references and index.
  ISBN 978-1-4846-0203-4 (hb)—ISBN 978-1-4846-0210-2
(pb) 1. Brachiosaurus—Juvenile literature. 2. Dinosaurs—
Juvenile literature. I. Title.

  QE862.S3N86 2015
  567.913—dc23   2013040463

Acknowledgments
We would like to thank the following for permission
to reproduce photographs: Alamy p. 11 (© Christian
Darkin); Corbis pp. 14, 15 (© Jim Zuckerman); Getty
Images pp. 18, 23 (Ulrich Baumgarten), 19 (Ken Lucas),
20 (Gamma-Rapho); Science Source pp. 6, 8 right
(Roger Harris); Shutterstock pp. 4, 7, 10, 13 (Kostyantyn
Ivanyshen), 5b (Audrey Snider-Bell), 5c (KAMONRAT),
5d (tratong), 8 left (James Steidl), 9 left (Bob Orsillo),
9 right (Hector Conesa), 9 scale (seesaw), 16 (Dereje),
23 (tratong); Superstock pp. 5a (Science Photo Library),
12 (imagebroker.net), 17 (Stocktrek Images), 21
(Louie Psihoyos).

Cover photograph of an adult brachiosaurus altithorax
on a beach in what is today North America, reproduced
with permission of Superstock (NHPA).

Back cover photograph of Brachiosaurus reprodcued
with permission of Shutterstock (Kostyantyn Ivanyshen).

We would like to thank Dee Reid and Nancy Harris for
their invaluable help in the preparation of this book.

Every effort has been made to contact copyright holders
of material reproduced in this book. Any omissions will
be rectified in subsequent printings if notice is given to
the publisher.

Contents

Meet Brachiosaurus

Brachiosaurus was a dinosaur.
Dinosaurs lived long ago.

dinosaur

crocodile

lizard

snake

Dinosaurs were reptiles.
Crocodiles, snakes, and lizards
are reptiles that live today.

What Was Brachiosaurus Like?

Brachiosaurus was a very big dinosaur.

Brachiosaurus had long legs.

Brachiosaurus was as tall as
a building with four floors!

Brachiosaurus was as heavy as 12 elephants!

tail

Brachiosaurus had a tail.

Brachiosaurus had a very long neck.

Brachiosaurus had a small head.

Brachiosaurus ate plants.

Brachiosaurus
had to eat
all day to get
enough food!

Brachiosaurus may have lived
for 100 years!

Where Is Brachiosaurus Now?

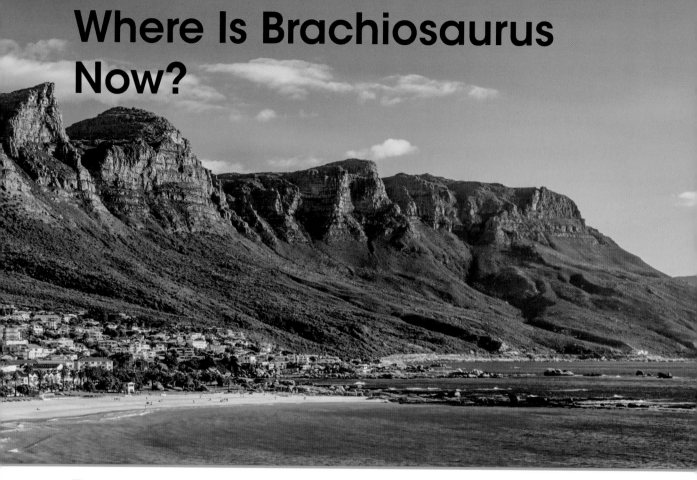

Brachiosaurus is extinct. There are no Brachiosaurus alive now.

All the dinosaurs died long ago.

We learn about Brachiosaurus
from fossils.

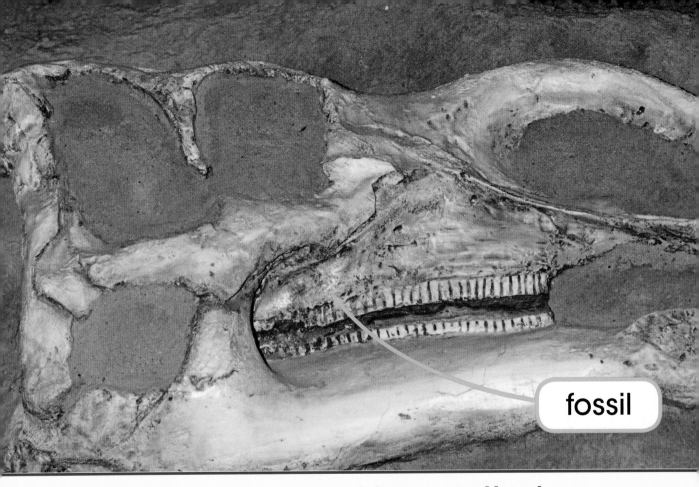

fossil

Fossils are animal bones that have turned to rock.

19

People find fossils in the ground.

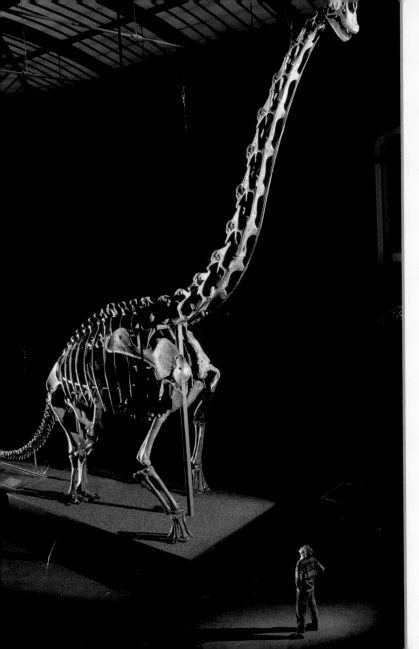

Fossils show
us what
Brachiosaurus
looked like.

Where In the World?

Brachiosaurus fossils have
been found in North America,
Europe, and Africa.

Picture Glossary

fossil animal bones or parts of a plant that have turned into rock

reptile cold-blooded animal. A lizard is a reptile.

How to Say It

Brachiosaurus: say
"brack-ee-uh-sawr-us"

Index

Notes for Parents and Teachers

Before Reading

Ask the children to name some dinosaurs. Ask them if dinosaurs are around today. Talk about how some dinosaurs ate plants and others ate other dinosaurs. Can they think of ways these dinosaurs might have been different? Have they heard of Brachiosaurus? Find out if they already know anything about this dinosaur.

After Reading

- Ask the children if they remember what a Brachiosaurus looked like—talk about its long neck and other physical characteristics. Make a Brachiosaurus collage together.
- Draw a four-story building and get the children to stick on bricks and windows. Then ask the children to guide you as you draw a picture of a Brachiosaurus next to the building. Now the children can stick on green and brown materials to decorate the Brachiosaurus.